Humanitarians

Carlotta Hacker

Crabtree Publishing Company

Dedication

This series is dedicated to every woman who has followed her dreams and to every young girl who hopes to do the same. While overcoming great odds and often oppression, the remarkable women in this series have triumphed in their fields. Their dedication, hard work, and excellence can serve as an inspiration to all—young and old, male and female. Women in Profile is both an acknowledgment of and a tribute to these great women.

Project Coordinator
Leslie Strudwick
Crabtree Editor
Virginia Mainprize
Editing and Proofreading
Alana Luft
Krista McLuskey
Lauri Seidlitz
Design
Warren Clark

Published by Crabtree Publishing Company

350 Fifth Avenue, Suite 3308
New York, NY
USA 10018

360 York Road, R.R. 4
Niagara-on-the-Lake
Ontario, Canada
L0S 1J0

Cataloging-in-Publication Data

Hacker, Carlotta.
      Humanitarians / Carlotta Hacker.
          p. cm. — (Women in profile)
      Includes bibliographical references and index.
      Summary: Traces the lives of six women who have devoted their lives to helping those in need, including Princess Diana, Dolores Huerta, Helen Keller, Graça Simbine Machel, Eleanor Roosevelt, and Mother Teresa.
      ISBN 0-7787-0011-9 (RLB) — ISBN-0-7787-0033-X (pbk.)
      1. Women social reformers—Biography—Juvenile literature.
2. Women social workers—Biography—Juvenile literature. 3. Women philanthropists—Biography—Juvenile literature. [1. Reformers.
2. Social workers. 3. Philanthropists. 4. Women—Biography.]
I. Title. II. Series.
HQ1123.H24 1999
305.4'092'2—dc21
                                      98-37060
                                          CIP
                                          AC

Photograph Credits
Every reasonable effort has been made to trace ownership and to obtain permission to reprint copyright material. The publishers would be pleased to have any errors or omissions brought to their attention so that they may be corrected in subsequent printings.

Archive Photos: cover, pages 9, 10, 17, 18, 20, 22, 30, 31, 32, 33, 36, 38, 39, 41, 44; Canapress Photo Service: page 11; The Cesar E. Chavez Foundation: pages 12, 13, 14; Corbis-Bettmann: page 35; Courtesy of Hadassah, The Women's Zionist Organization of Canada: page 45; Image Works: pages 6, 7, 8, 24, 28, 29, 40, 42; Photofest: pages 19, 23, 34; Save the Children Fund: Page 43; UN Photo 188807 (E. Schneider): page 26; UPI/Corbis-Bettmann: pages 15, 16, 21, 27.

Contents

Humanitarians

A humanitarian is someone who cares what happens to others and helps them when they are in need. Humanitarians do not expect anything in return. They are pleased if someone says "Thank you," but they do not expect to be paid or given a reward. They do what they do because they want to make the world a better place.

Anyone can be a humanitarian. Some people do volunteer work in the evenings after a busy day at the office or factory. Some coach people with disabilities to help them become better athletes. Others take meals to elderly people living alone. Young people sometimes help out in hospitals as "candystripers." All these people are behaving as humanitarians. So is the student who is kind to a lonely girl or boy.

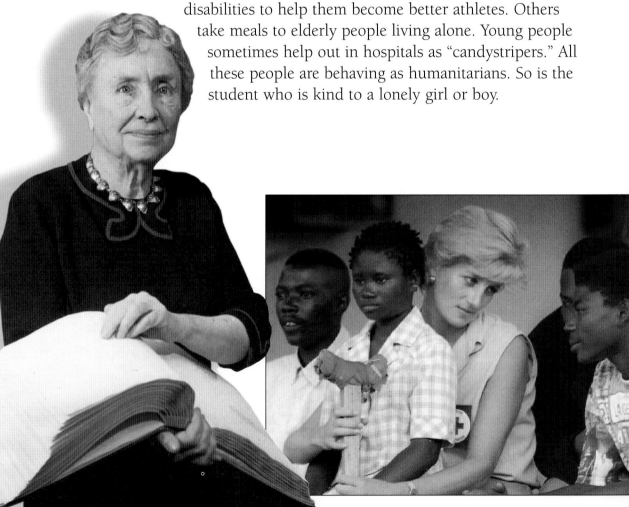

The six women whose stories are told in this book are great humanitarians. They have helped many people. All have lived very different lives from one another, yet they have one thing in common—their concern for others. Some of them have devoted their lives to helping the needy.

More women humanitarians are described briefly at the end of the book. There you will discover more ways in which people can help others.

As you read these stories, think about your own life. Are you a humanitarian? Would you like to be one? Many university students go overseas for a year or two to help in faraway countries. Others raise funds at home for people in need. You do not have to wait until you are older to be a humanitarian. There are sure to be people in your community who could use your helping hand. There may even be people in your school who need help. Even small acts of kindness can make the world a better place, and you a humanitarian.

"Being permanently in the public eye gives me a special responsibility, that of using the impact of photographs to get a message across, a message about an important cause or certain values."

Diana, Princess of Wales

Supporter of the Sick and Disadvantaged

Early Years

When Diana was little, she seemed to have everything any child could want. Her family was very wealthy. Her home in Norfolk, England, had a heated swimming pool. She had plenty of toys and even a pony. But there was one thing Diana did not have, her mother.

Diana's parents had separated when she was six, and her mother had left home. Diana missed her mother a lot. Although Diana's father was still at home, she did not see him much. Like her brother and sisters, she was looked after mostly by servants.

When Diana was nine, she was sent to boarding school. At first, she was lonely, even though she was allowed to keep her pet guinea pig, Peanuts, at the school. A few years later, her father moved the family to a house called Althorp. Althorp was huge, more like a castle than a house, and Diana felt lost there. She felt even more lost when her father married again.

Diana with her younger brother, Charles. He is the godson of Queen Elizabeth II.

BACKGROUNDER

Diana's Family

Diana's family have been **aristocrats** for hundreds of years. When Diana's grandfather died in 1975, her father became Earl Spencer. He inherited this title from his father. He also inherited Althorp, the family estate in Northamptonshire. From then on, Diana was known as Lady Diana Spencer, and her two older sisters became Lady Jane and Lady Sarah. Her younger brother, Charles, became Viscount Althorp. He is now called Earl Spencer, after inheriting the title when his father died in 1991. Diana's mother, Frances, is also an aristocrat. Her father was Lord Fermoy.

Developing Skills

The house in Norfolk, where Diana spent her early childhood, stood in the same park as Sandringham House, the Queen's country house. Diana was used to being with the Royal Family. She called the Queen "Aunt Lilibet" and was friendly with the younger princes, Andrew and Edward. They often came to swim in her family's pool. Since Prince Charles was older, he was not one of Diana's friends at Sandringham. Diana did not really get to know him until 1977, when he was invited to Althorp to shoot pheasants. Diana was sixteen at the time. Charles was twenty-nine and had been dating Diana's older sister, Sarah. He and Diana were immediately attracted to each other.

During the next three years, their romance blossomed. At first, it was kept secret, but soon the media found out. From then on, Diana was trailed by photographers. One photographer even took a picture of her at the kindergarten where she taught. When Diana tried to hide from the cameras, the media called her "Shy Di."

When her mother remarried, Diana would travel to Scotland to visit her.

Charles and Diana were married in July, 1981, in a splendid ceremony that was shown on television all over the world. People called it a "fairy-tale wedding" and talked about the "happy couple," but the couple was not especially happy. Although they thought they were in love, they had different interests. Diana liked pop music. Charles liked classical. Charles liked to read serious books. Diana did not. In fact, they had very little in common.

As the months passed, Diana became more and more unhappy. She felt cut off from the world. As Princess of Wales, she had very little private life. She could not go shopping or even take a walk without attracting a crowd.

*"I don't want to be **patron** of a charity unless I can get involved in it. Nothing would upset me more than just being a name on the top of a piece of paper.... I long to help in all sorts of areas."*

The birth of Diana's sons, William and Harry, made her happier, but she still had problems. She stopped eating properly and became very thin. Meanwhile, she smiled and waved at the crowds as she carried out her duties as a princess. Although Diana smiled in public, she often felt like crying. She wanted to do more with her life than just be a princess.

Within a year of her marriage, over a dozen biographies had been written about Diana. People wanted to know as much as they could about the princess.

"You can shake hands with people with AIDS and give them a hug. Heaven knows, they need it."

Accomplishments

Diana was a loving mother and was often seen hugging her sons and showing them lots of affection. People began to notice that she behaved the same way with other children. When she visited a hospital, she picked up children and cradled them in her arms. Diana hated to see children in pain.

Diana showed the same sympathy for anyone who was sick. When she had a choice of functions to attend, she would visit a hospital rather than a theater. The patients were always thrilled to meet her. "She's so easy to talk to," they said. They liked the way she held their hands while listening to their problems. It was so friendly and casual.

In 1987, Diana visited nine men who were dying of **AIDS** in a London hospital. She shook hands with them and sat on their beds and chatted. By touching the men, Diana showed the world that people with AIDS should not be feared. She was saying that you could not catch the disease just by touching. That day, Diana did more good for AIDS patients than all the experts who had been trying to spread the same message.

By the early 1990s, Diana was patron of more than ninety charities. She comforted cancer patients, visited homes for battered women, and talked to teenagers about drug abuse. Without realizing it, she had become far more than a princess. She had used her position to help people in need.

Diana visited many people in hospitals, especially children.

Unfortunately, Diana's marriage was not going as well as her charities. She and Charles had grown more apart each year, and in 1992 they formally separated. They were divorced in 1996.

Hoping to be treated as a private person once again, Diana dropped much of her charity work, but she was soon involved in a new cause—**landmines**. In 1997, she visited Angola and Bosnia to draw attention to the dangers of the mines. That was Diana's last effort. On August 31, she and her friend Dodi Fayed were killed in a car crash in France when fleeing from the paparazzi who were chasing them. That night, the world lost its "Queen of Hearts," and the sick and suffering lost one of their greatest supporters.

Quick Notes

- **Althorp has belonged to Diana's family for almost five hundred years.**

- **More than 700 million people watched Diana's wedding on television.**

- **Many people felt that Diana had been "hounded to death" by the paparazzi. Her brother said, "I always believed that the press would kill her in the end."**

- **At Diana's funeral, Elton John performed a special version of his song "Candle in the Wind." It included the words "Goodbye, England's rose."**

- **Diana is buried on an island in a lake at Althorp.**

Diana traveled to Angola, an African country, to visit the victims of landmines.

"I think we brought to the United States the idea of boycotting as a non-violent tactic.... We showed that non-violence can work to make social change."

Dolores Huerta

American Farm Labor Leader

Early Years

Dolores's grandfather called her "seven tongues" because she talked so much. She was a little chatterbox, he said. Dolores loved her grandfather. She and her two brothers were raised by him in Stockton, California.

Dolores's parents had split up in 1935, when she was five years old, and she seldom saw her father during her childhood. He had stayed in New Mexico when her mother took the family to California. Dolores's mother supported them all by working as a waitress and a cook. Later, she opened her own small hotel and restaurant in Stockton.

During the school holidays, Dolores and her brothers helped in the restaurant. Dolores's mother was very kind. She sometimes let **migrant** farm workers and their families stay in the hotel without paying. "They earn so little that they need every penny," she said. Eager to follow her mother's example, Dolores joined a group that helped farm workers' families.

Backgrounder

Farm Workers

Many of the workers on California's farms are immigrants from Mexico and other Spanish-speaking countries. Some of them cannot speak English. They pick fruit by hand and are paid very little. Although they work long hours in the fields, they earn far less than most Americans. For many years, they did not dare to complain. They were sure that the powerful owners of the fruit farms would not listen to them, and many were frightened of losing their jobs. In other jobs, workers can usually join a **union** to bargain with their employers, but there was no union for farm workers in the 1950s.

Developing Skills

After Dolores left school, she worked in a grocery store. A few years later, she got a job as a secretary. Meanwhile, she married and had two children. The marriage was not a success. Soon, she was on her own again.

Dolores enrolled at Stockton College and trained to be a teacher while her mother looked after Dolores's children. Teaching seemed a good way of helping others, but it almost broke Dolores's heart. "I couldn't stand seeing kids come to class hungry and needing shoes," she said.

Most of the students were children of farm laborers, who worked long hours for very low wages. Dolores decided that she would be of more use to the children if she could find a way of getting their parents' wages raised or of improving their lives.

In 1955, Dolores met Fred Ross, who worked for the Community Service Organization (CSO). Fred told her how the CSO had worked with the Spanish-speaking people of Los Angeles to improve their living conditions. The CSO had helped to set up educational programs, open childcare centers, and build health clinics. "I felt like I had found a pot of gold," said Dolores. She and Fred immediately started a branch of the CSO in Stockton.

"I thought I could do more by organizing farm workers than by trying to teach their hungry children."

Through the CSO, Dolores met César Chávez, one of the group's leaders. Like Dolores, César wanted to help the farm workers. He thought the best way would be to form a union. The union's leaders could meet with the employers to demand higher pay and better working conditions.

In 1962, Dolores and César formed a union called the National Farm Workers' Association. Their friends thought they were crazy. "How are you going to organize farm workers?" they asked. "Farm workers are poor immigrants. They don't have any power. They can't even vote." Dolores and César knew that the farm workers were powerless, but that was why they wanted them to form a union. If enough workers banded together, they would be able to force the farm owners to listen to their requests.

Dolores (far right) meeting with farm workers.

BACKGROUNDER

The Farm Workers' Union

When the National Farm Workers' Association was formed in 1962, César Chávez became president, with Dolores as vice-president. Dolores remained vice-president until 1993, though the union underwent several changes during those years. In 1966, it joined with two other unions to become the United Farm Workers' Organizing Committee. In 1972, it became the United Farm Workers of America. At that time, the union had 80,000 members. After Dolores retired from the position of vice-president in 1993, she continued to work for the union.

Accomplishments

During the next few years, more than a thousand fruit pickers joined the National Farm Workers' Association. In 1965, the union supported a group of grape pickers who went on **strike** for better pay and other improved working conditions. The strike lasted five years, spreading throughout California as more and more farm laborers stopped working.

Dolores and the other union leaders made sure the public knew why the workers were striking. They described the terrible working conditions, the low pay, and the danger of being poisoned by the **pesticides** sprayed on the grapes. They pointed out that grape pickers did not get sick leave or any of the other benefits available in most jobs. They were treated almost like slaves.

Shocked by what they heard, many people throughout the country supported the strikers. A few of the grape-growing companies offered the workers a raise in pay and promised to give them health care and protection from dangerous chemicals.

Dolores, César, and their supporters often marched to attract public attention to the working conditions of farm laborers.

However, most grape growers refused to make any changes. The union declared a **boycott**, asking the public not to buy grapes grown by these companies. Dolores led the boycott in Washington, appearing on talk shows and radio programs. It was one of the most successful boycotts in history.

So many people refused to buy Californian grapes that the companies found they were losing money. They realized that if they wanted to stay in business, they would have to meet the union's demands. They met with Dolores in 1970 and signed contracts stating how workers would be treated and paid. These contracts at last gave grape pickers many of the same benefits that other workers had long taken for granted.

Since then, Dolores has led other successful strikes and has tried to get laws passed to protect other farm workers. She was pleased in 1975 when California passed the Agricultural Labor Relations Act.

In recent years, Dolores has been honored with several awards. She feels proud to be so honored, but she is even more proud of the songs her people sing about her. Mexican Americans have written ballads about Dolores, telling how she has spent her life trying to improve the lives of others.

Quick Notes

- Dolores has often been called Dolores Huelga (*huelga* means "strike" in Spanish).

- After Dolores grew up, she got to know her father, who was an active union leader.

- Dolores had eleven children: seven girls and four boys.

- Dolores believed in peaceful protests without any violence.

- During a protest in 1988, Dolores was knocked to the ground by a police officer. Several of her ribs were broken, and she was hurt so badly that her doctors thought she might die.

"We have laid a pattern of how farm workers are eventually going to get out of their bondage."

Dolores supported the work of other groups. She is shown (third from the right) marching for the National Organization of Women.

"Everyone who wishes to gain true knowledge must climb Hill Difficulty alone.... I slip back many times. I run against hidden obstacles. I lose my temper, find it again, keep it better, and trudge on.... Every struggle is a victory."

Helen Keller

American Author and Lecturer

Early Years

Can you imagine not being able to see and hear? Shut your eyes for a moment and cover your ears. That is what life was like for Helen. When she was nineteen months old, she had a severe illness that left her blind and deaf.

Helen had just begun to talk when she fell sick, but she stopped talking when she lost her hearing. Since she could not hear people speaking, words meant nothing to her. The only word she still used was "water." She said "wa-wa" when she was thirsty. Otherwise, she used signs to show what she wanted. Often, people did not understand. This made Helen mad. She got so angry that she sometimes kicked furniture and broke things.

Helen's parents realized she felt desperate, but they could do little to help. In the 1880s, there was no school for children like Helen near their home in Tuscumbia, Alabama.

BACKGROUNDER

Helen's Family

Helen was the oldest child in the family. She had a younger brother and sister. Her parents, Arthur and Kate Keller, were well-educated people who thought learning was very important. Helen's father was the publisher of a weekly newspaper.

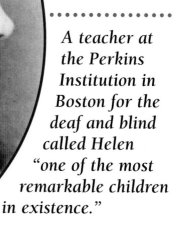

A teacher at the Perkins Institution in Boston for the deaf and blind called Helen "one of the most remarkable children in existence."

BACKGROUNDER

The Manual Alphabet and Braille

Helen was often asked how she understood what people said to her. She explained: "The person who reads or talks to me spells with his hand.... I place my hand on the hand of the speaker so lightly as not to impede its movements. The position of the hand is as easy to feel as it is to see." When Helen was attending lectures at Radcliffe College, Anne sat beside her and told her manually everything the lecturer was saying. Helen was also taught to read braille. This is a form of printing for the blind. The letters of the alphabet are formed by raised dots that can easily be felt with a finger. When Helen wanted to write something, she used either a braille machine or a typewriter.

Helen could "hear" Anne by feeling vibrations on her lips.

Developing Skills

W hen Helen was six, her parents took her to see a specialist in Boston. With his help, they hired a **governess** who had been trained to teach deaf children. Her name was Anne Sullivan.

Anne had almost lost her own sight some years earlier, so she understood how Helen felt. The day Anne arrived, she gave Helen a doll. Then she placed Helen's hand on her own and wrote with her fingers "d-o-l-l." Anne continued to do this until Helen could do the same without help. Although Helen did not realize it, she was being taught the "manual alphabet."

Over the next few days, Helen learned to write other words. She enjoyed this new game, but she thought it was only a game. She did not realize that the words meant something. Then, about two weeks later, Anne poured some water over Helen's hand while writing "water" with the other hand. Suddenly, a wonderful thought came to Helen: "I realized that everything has a name." It opened a whole new world to her.

"I knew then that 'w-a-t-e-r' meant the wonderful cool something that was flowing over my hand."

From then on, Helen wanted to know the name of everything. She was so eager that she learned very quickly. In the next few months, she learned hundreds of words, and soon she was able to write sentences too. Helen took another big step forward when she started writing letters. She wrote to everyone she could think of, her parents, her sister, and all her relatives.

In less than a year, Helen and Anne could "talk" to each other without difficulty. Anne then began to educate Helen. She taught her history, geography, French, and even Latin. Each subject gave Helen a wider view of the world around her.

Still Helen wanted more. She wanted to be able to speak— really speak. She knew that was how other people communicated. She had put her hand on their lips and throat and felt them talking. A specialist showed Helen how to make the necessary sounds, but she never managed to speak clearly. Anne could understand her, and so could her family, but most people could not.

Meanwhile, Helen continued her education. She made such good progress that she was accepted by Radcliffe College in Cambridge, Massachusetts. She graduated with honors in 1904.

Even before she finished college, Helen had written a book that was translated into fifty languages.

Accomplishments

While Helen was a student at Radcliffe, she wrote a book called *The Story of My Life*. It made her famous. People were amazed that a young woman who was both deaf and blind could achieve so much. They wanted to meet Helen and see her for themselves, so she began to appear in public. She traveled from city to city, giving lectures with Anne acting as interpreter. These tours made Helen even more famous.

Helen used her fame to help others. When appearing in public, she described the special needs of the blind, and she asked her audiences to give money to help them. As a result, the newly formed American Foundation for the Blind began to receive huge sums of money.

Next, Helen turned her attention to the poorer people of America. She sided with workers who went on **strike** for higher pay. She tried to get laws passed to prevent children from working on plantations and in factories. She supported the National Association for the Advancement of Colored People, an organization trying to improve the lives of African Americans.

Helen gave lectures about the special needs of the blind.

These efforts caused some people to turn against Helen. Some of her relatives were furious that she was siding with African Americans. They did not want African Americans to have the same privileges they had. Other people objected to Helen's **socialism**. She should not encourage workers to strike, they said.

None of these criticisms stopped Helen from supporting her causes. She had her biggest success in the 1930s, when she persuaded Congress to pass laws on behalf of the blind. These laws provided free reading services, "talking books," and other aids for blind people.

When Helen was in her fifties, she began to travel abroad, hoping to make life better for blind people in other countries. She went to Japan, South Africa, and many other places. Wherever she went, many people came to see her. Because of Helen's efforts, life was made easier and more comfortable for blind people in many parts of the world.

Quick Notes

- Even before Anne arrived as her governess, Helen had invented more than sixty signs and gestures to show people what she wanted.

- Helen wrote several books and many articles.

- Helen helped make two films about her life: *Deliverance* (1918) and *The Unconquered* (1954).

- Helen received many honors, including the Presidential Medal of Freedom (1964).

- Alexander Graham Bell, the inventor of the telephone, was a specialist who taught deaf people to speak. He first met Helen when she was six and gave her a lot of encouragement over the years.

"I will always, as long as I have breath, work for the handicapped."

*"Self-reliance is the best
lesson we can learn."*

Graça Simbine Machel

Mozambican Children's Rights Advocate

Early Years

Just twenty days after her father died, Graça was born. That was why she was called Graça. It means for the grace of God. Her mother felt that, in spite of their tragedy, her baby would make the family happy again.

Graça lived in a small village in Mozambique. Her home was a round mud hut with a grass roof. Although Graça's mother had very little money, she saved enough to send Graça to primary school. Relatives helped pay for Graça to go to secondary school.

Graça knew that her relatives were going short of things so that she could get an education. To thank them, she worked very hard at school. She did so well that in 1968 she won a scholarship to study at Lisbon University in Portugal.

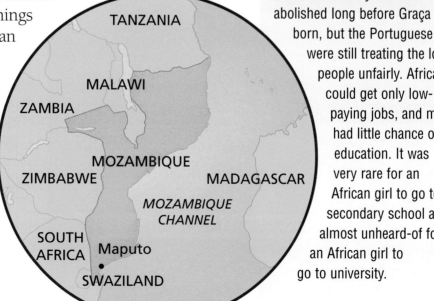

TANZANIA

MALAWI

ZAMBIA

MOZAMBIQUE

ZIMBABWE

MADAGASCAR

MOZAMBIQUE CHANNEL

SOUTH AFRICA

Maputo

SWAZILAND

BACKGROUNDER

A Portuguese Colony

When Graça was growing up, Mozambique was a **colony**, called Portuguese East Africa. The Portuguese explorer Vasco da Gama had landed there in 1498 and claimed the land for Portugal. Da Gama was followed by Portuguese traders, who took away all the ivory and gold they could find. They also seized many Africans and sold them as slaves. Slavery had been abolished long before Graça was born, but the Portuguese were still treating the local people unfairly. Africans could get only low-paying jobs, and most had little chance of an education. It was very rare for an African girl to go to secondary school and almost unheard-of for an African girl to go to university.

Developing Skills

At Lisbon University, Graça met African students who wanted to bring an end to Portuguese rule in Mozambique. They said it was time Africans ran their own government. Graça agreed. Many former British colonies were now independent countries governed by Africans. The same thing should happen in Mozambique, she said.

Some of the students belonged to a group called FRELIMO, which was already fighting the Portuguese in some parts of Mozambique. While Graça was at the university, she decided to join FRELIMO. "We had to pretend we were having parties," she later said. "We played music very loud and pretended we were dancing. But really we were discussing politics."

When Graça returned home in 1973, the fighting had spread, and there was open war in Mozambique. Graça went to the neighboring country of Tanzania for military training so that she could help in the fight for freedom. In the end, she did more teaching than fighting. She was made assistant head of a secondary school where children of FRELIMO soldiers were educated.

Graça was not afraid to speak out for her beliefs.

While working in Tanzania, Graça Simbine met Samora Machel, the leader of FRELIMO. The two were married in 1975. That same year, Mozambique gained independence from Portugal. Samora became president of the new country, and Graça became minister of education and culture.

One of FRELIMO's aims was to give every child in Mozambique a good education. It was Graça's job to make this happen. She tackled the task with enthusiasm, for she knew how important education was. Growing up in her village, she had known many people who could not even write their own names. Because they could not read and write, they had difficulty getting jobs.

During the next few years, Graça changed education in Mozambique. She arranged for new schools to be built throughout the country. She hired teachers and met with them to discuss what they would teach. Before long, even children in remote villages could go to school. Many adults also went to school, taking their lessons in the evenings.

Much of Graça's work was undone in the 1980s, when Mozambique was plunged into another war. The war caused chaos throughout the country.

BACKGROUNDER
FRELIMO's Struggle for Independence

FRELIMO began its struggle against Portuguese rule in the early 1960s. It was opposed by the Portuguese army, and there was bitter fighting. By the early 1970s, FRELIMO had gained control of much of the country. The war ended in 1974, and Mozambique became independent from Portugal in January 1975.

"The base of human behavior is solidarity, love, and mutual assistance—starting with the family."

Graça traveled all over the world with her husband. Here she is shaking hands with President Mitterand of France while Samora looks on.

BACKGROUNDER

Another War in Mozambique

The FRELIMO government of Samora Machel was run on **communist** lines. One of the first things it did was take away the land owned by Portuguese farmers. Many of the Portuguese fled to South Africa, where there was widespread fear of communism. Aided by South Africa, Rhodesia (now known as Zimbabwe), and the United States, a group called RENAMO, which was against Samora Machel's government, began a war against FRELIMO. During the 1980s, RENAMO fighters attacked schools and hospitals, and burned villages. More than two million people were made homeless, and thousands of children were orphaned. The war came to an end in 1992. FRELIMO agreed to hold elections in which all the people of Mozambique could choose their government.

Graça with her daughters at her husband's funeral.

Accomplishments

As **civil war** spread across Mozambique, Graça struggled to keep the schools open. It was a losing battle. She gave up her efforts in 1986, when her husband was killed in a plane crash which many believe was set up by his enemies. Graça was heartbroken. She left her job as government minister, and for the next five years, she wore only black.

In 1991, Graça's twelve-year-old son told his mother he could not remember her wearing cheerful clothing. This made Graça realize she should not spend the rest of her life mourning for her husband. There were more positive things she could do.

One of the first things Graça did was help the children who had been orphaned in the war. Hundreds of thousands of children had lost their parents in the fighting. Graça found new homes for many of them.

Graça also helped adults. In 1992, she formed the Foundation for Community Development of Mozambique. This group, which is funded largely by Americans, helps people start projects that will improve their own communities. This work may involve building a pipeline to supply water for a community's crops, or it may be something much bigger.

In 1993, Graça was appointed United Nations special expert on children and warfare. As part of this job, she studied how children are harmed by war. Graça hoped that by showing the world how much children suffer, she could persuade people to protect them and keep them out of the fighting.

While doing all this work, Graça tries to get people to forget the years of warfare in Mozambique and to live in peace. "We know that the RENAMO fighters have killed thousands of people," she says, "but we are not going to kill them. We'll bring them back into society and try to make them normal people again."

This attitude of forgiveness is very similar to that of Nelson Mandela, the president of South Africa. He and Graça became close companions and in July, 1998, they married.

Quick Notes

- **Graça is pronounced Grassa.**

- **The village where Graça was born is about 100 miles (160 kilometers) north of Maputo, the capital of Mozambique.**

- **Graça and Samora had two children. Graça also brought up Samora's family of six children from a previous marriage.**

- **Graça's many awards include the Nansen Medal for doing outstanding work for refugee children.**

"We try to help children become children again— to do the things normal children do."

Graça with her husband Nelson Mandela.

"We do not have to become heroes overnight. Just one step at a time, meeting each thing that comes up, seeing it is not as dreadful as it appears."

Eleanor Roosevelt

American Social Reformer

Early Years

Eleanor was born into a wealthy family, but she had a miserable childhood. She never believed her mother loved her. Eleanor's mother was very beautiful, and Eleanor was not. "It's a pity you are so plain," her mother told her.

The only person who made a fuss over Eleanor was her father, but he died when she was ten. By then, one of her brothers and her mother had also died. Eleanor and her remaining brother were sent to live with their grandmother.

Eleanor was lonely at her grandmother's. Her brother was too young to be a companion, and she had no friends her own age. Instead of going to school with other children, she was taught at home. At last in 1902, when Eleanor was fifteen, she was sent to a boarding school in England. "Those were the happiest years of my life," she once said.

BACKGROUNDER

The Roosevelt Family

Eleanor's full name was Anna Eleanor Roosevelt. She was born in New York City, the daughter of Elliott and Anna Roosevelt. Her uncle Theodore Roosevelt was the twenty-sixth president of the United States. Eleanor later married her fifth cousin Franklin Delano Roosevelt, who became the thirty-second president.

Eleanor spent a lot of time alone when she was a young girl.

Developing Skills

At Allenswood school in England, Eleanor learned more than the usual school subjects. She was taught that rich people have a duty to help those in need. It was a lesson she never forgot.

When Eleanor returned home at the age of seventeen, she began to help the poor in New York City. She gave exercise classes at a settlement house, a place that offered help to those in need. She also joined a group that was trying to make life better for women factory workers.

Eleanor had to stop this work when she married her cousin Franklin in 1905. Franklin's mother was afraid Eleanor would catch a disease from the people at the settlement house and spread it to her family. In any case, Eleanor was soon busy bringing up her own children, a daughter and four sons.

Eleanor and Franklin Roosevelt were married on March 17, 1905. They chose that date so that Eleanor's uncle President Theodore Roosevelt would be able to walk Eleanor down the aisle.

When the United States joined World War I in 1917, Eleanor was able to take up social work again. She and Franklin were living in Washington D.C. at the time. Each morning, Eleanor got up at five o'clock to go to Washington's Union Station. There she helped feed soldiers who were on their way to training camps. Eleanor also visited wounded soldiers in the hospital. After the war, she went back to doing social work for women. Among other things, she tried to get the laws changed to make factory owners pay women better wages.

In 1921, Eleanor's life was suddenly turned upside down—Franklin caught **polio**. This disease was killing many people at the time. Franklin did not die, but his legs were paralyzed. He could not walk. He eventually was able to take a few steps with the aid of two sticks, but it was very tiring. Most of the time, he was pushed in a wheelchair or carried.

Franklin was a politician who needed to be out meeting the public. How could he continue his work? Eleanor solved the problem by taking over many of his responsibilities. On his behalf, she talked with a wide range of voters and led a group to the Democratic party's national convention in 1924. Four years later, Eleanor again campaigned on Franklin's behalf. It was partly due to her efforts that he was elected governor of New York state in 1928, and again in 1930. In 1932, Franklin was elected president of the United States.

BACKGROUNDER

Franklin Delano Roosevelt

Franklin was a member of the Democratic party. He began his political career in 1910, when he was elected to the senate of New York state. From 1913 to 1920, he worked for the federal government as assistant secretary to the navy. Returning to New York politics in 1928, Franklin was elected state governor. He was first elected president of the United States in 1932. Franklin served as president from 1933 until his death in 1945. At that time, a president was allowed to serve more than two terms in office. Franklin was elected four times—in 1932, 1936, 1940, and 1944.

"The thing always to remember is to do the thing you think you cannot do."

While Franklin was president, Eleanor served as first lady for thirteen years.

Accomplishments

When her husband was sworn into office in 1933, Eleanor became first lady. In this position, she had the opportunity to do a great deal of good for people throughout the country. During the next few years, Eleanor traveled around the United States so that she could see for herself how people were living. She visited coal mines and factories, hospitals and schools. When she returned to Washington, she told the president what she had seen.

In the 1930s, many people were out of work because of the Great Depression. Although he tried, Franklin could not solve all the country's problems. However, because of Eleanor's efforts, he heard about the people who were suffering most, and he did what he could to help them.

"How to preserve the freedoms of democracy in the world.... These are the questions the youth of today must face, and we who are older must face them too."

Eleanor gave speeches and radio broadcasts about the state of the country. Since she so obviously cared about those in need, many people wrote to her asking for help. Eleanor always answered their letters, and if she could do something, she always did.

Eleanor was particularly concerned about the way many white Americans treated African Americans. In 1939, a group of women, called the Daughters of the American Revolution, refused to let the great African-American singer, Marian Anderson, perform in their hall. Eleanor was so angry that she resigned from the group. She arranged for Marian to give an outdoor concert at the Lincoln Memorial in Washington.

When Franklin died in 1945, Eleanor lost her position as first lady, but she did not lose her influence. People still turned to her for help, knowing that she would take up their cause. During Eleanor's final years, she worked hard for world peace. She visited many countries to talk about living together in friendship. People listened to what Eleanor said. They had the greatest respect for her. She had become a first lady of the world.

Quick Notes

- **Starting in 1936, Eleanor wrote a newspaper column called "My Day."**

- **Eleanor sometimes invited garment workers and other low-paid people to have dinner at the White House. She sat them next to the president so that they could tell him about their problems.**

- **Eleanor did a lot of work with the American Student Union and other youth groups.**

- **After World War II, Eleanor was appointed a delegate to the United Nations. She helped draw up the Universal Declaration of Human Rights.**

Even after her husband's death, Eleanor continued to put pressure on politicians to promote human rights.

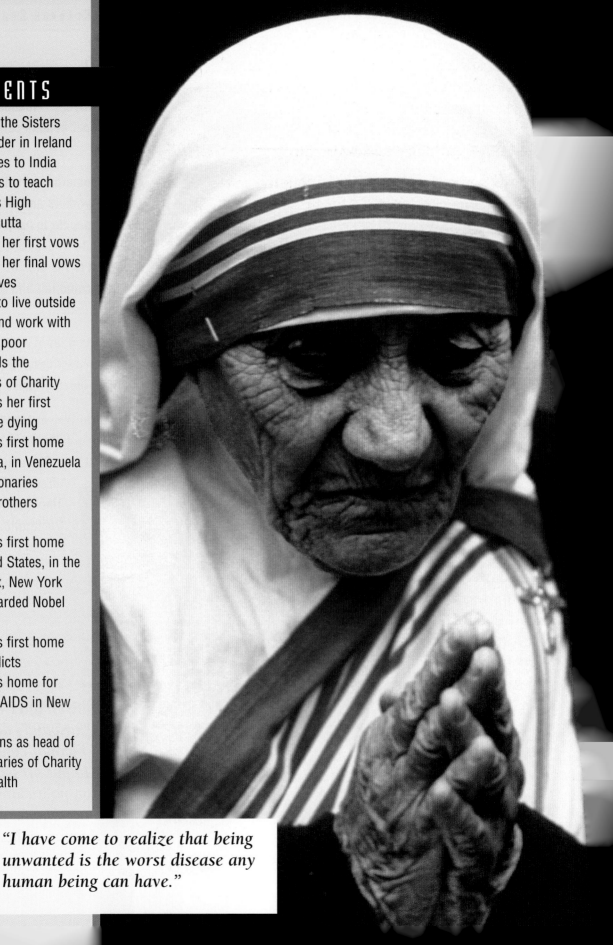

KEY EVENTS

1928 Joins the Sisters of Loreto order in Ireland and then goes to India
1929 Begins to teach at St. Mary's High School, Calcutta
1931 Takes her first vows
1937 Takes her final vows
1948 Receives permission to live outside St. Mary's and work with the Calcutta poor
1950 Founds the Missionaries of Charity
1952 Opens her first home for the dying
1965 Opens first home outside India, in Venezuela
1966 Missionaries of Charity Brothers are formed
1971 Opens first home in the United States, in the South Bronx, New York
1979 Is awarded Nobel Peace Prize
1980 Opens first home for drug addicts
1985 Opens home for people with AIDS in New York City
1997 Resigns as head of the Missionaries of Charity due to ill health

"I have come to realize that being unwanted is the worst disease any human being can have."

Mother Teresa

Albanian Roman Catholic Missionary

Early Years

Mother Teresa was born in the town of Skopje, Albania, which is now part of Macedonia. Her name was Agnes Gonxha Bojaxhiu, and her father was a builder. She had one brother and one sister. When Agnes was nine, her father died, and the family lost all its money. Her mother sewed clothes for other people to support her children.

Like many people in Skopje, Agnes's family was Roman Catholic. As a child, she was often told about the work of Catholic missionaries in faraway countries. Agnes listened to the stories eagerly. "At the age of twelve, I first knew I had a calling to help the poor," she has said. "I wanted to be a missionary." She decided that she would go to India. It had many people who needed help.

BACKGROUNDER

Missionaries

Missionaries are people who are sent by their church to teach religion in another country. They may also run schools and hospitals. Some Roman Catholic missionaries are nuns. These women dedicate their lives to God and usually live together in a community. They take vows, promising never to marry and to have no personal belongings.

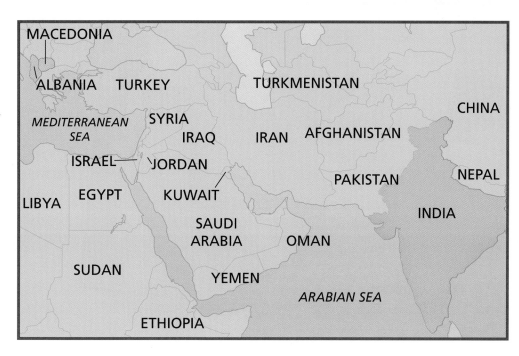

Developing Skills

When Agnes was eighteen, she joined an order of nuns called the Sisters of Loreto who worked in Calcutta, one of the biggest cities in India. She took the name Sister Teresa.

Sister Teresa was appointed a teacher at St. Mary's, a Roman Catholic high school for girls in Calcutta. She taught there for almost twenty years and was made principal of the school.

St. Mary's was also a **convent**. It was a large stone building with beautiful gardens. From her bedroom window, Teresa could see the nearest bustee, the slum of tin-roofed huts where the very poor people lived. The sight upset her more and more. It was terrible that so many people were living in such misery, with nobody to give them help or even comfort.

Mother Teresa hands out rice and blankets to the needy of Calcutta.

By 1946, Teresa was sure that God was telling her to help the people in the bustee. "The message was clear. I was to leave the convent and help the poor, while living among them." Living among the poor was an unusual thing for a nun to do. Teresa had to get permission from the church authorities in order to leave the convent.

Two years passed before permission was granted. Before Teresa started her work in the slum, she took a medical course so that she could treat the sick. Then she went into the bustee. She had no money and no real plan, but she believed God would help her. She gathered together a group of children whom she began to teach in a vacant lot. She had no blackboard or books. Using a stick, she drew the letters of the Bengali alphabet in the earth.

At first, some of the people in the bustee made fun of Teresa. A few even threw stones. They feared she was trying to convert the children from their Hindu religion and make them become Christians. As time passed, they changed their minds. They saw that Teresa was helping in all sorts of ways. She brought the children soap and small parcels of food. She bandaged people's wounds and gave medicine to the sick—and she never asked for anything in return.

"I had a call from God to give up everything and go into the slums to serve the poorest of the poor."

BACKGROUNDER
India

More than 950 million people live in India. It is one of the most densely populated countries in the world. The cities are particularly crowded. In Calcutta, there are more than twelve million people, many without homes. They sleep on the sidewalk or in the gutter at the side of the road. Some of those who do have homes are not much better off. Whole families live in one-room shacks in crowded slums. If they want to wash or get a drink of water, they walk to an outside tap that they share with other families. Disease spreads easily in these conditions. Since the people in the slums cannot afford a doctor, many of them die of their diseases.

Mother Teresa's Missionaries of Charity were to serve the poorest of the poor.

Accomplishments

Before long, some former students from St. Mary's school joined Teresa in her work. Most of them were Indian girls from wealthy homes. In 1950, the group became known as the Missionaries of Charity, a new community of nuns. As head of the community, Teresa was now called "Mother."

Two years later, the city of Calcutta gave Mother Teresa two rooms behind a Hindu temple. These small rooms became her first hostel, where she cared for the dying. In Calcutta, when very poor people are sick, they have nowhere to go. Some just lie down and die on the street. The Missionaries of Charity brought these homeless, sick people to the hostel and nursed them. Even if they could not be cured, they could still be cared for lovingly. "They have lived like animals," said Mother Teresa. "At least they can die like angels."

As word spread about the Missionaries of Charity, more and more women wanted to join, and more and more people gave money to the cause. Soon, Mother Teresa was able to open hostels for the dying in other Indian cities and in other countries. She also started schools and orphanages. Wherever Mother Teresa saw a need, she tried to fill it.

In 1979, Mother Teresa was awarded the Nobel Peace Prize. This made her even better known and brought her many more followers. Some people criticized her, however. They said she was using a "band-aid" approach—just patching things up instead of changing society so that people would not be poor and helpless.

Mother Teresa took no notice of these complaints. She explained that she was serving God who had called her to do this work. "I have been called to help the individual," she said. "I have not been called to deal with institutions. I am not trying to change anything." In fact, Mother Teresa has changed things. She and her Missionaries of Charity have brought peace and comfort to thousands of people around the world.

Quick Notes

- **Mother Teresa has been called the Saint of the Gutters.**

- **Mother Teresa wrote *Gift for God* (1975), *A Simple Path* (1995), and several other books.**

- **In 1949, Mother Teresa became an Indian citizen.**

- **Mother Teresa was given an honorary degree in medicine by the Catholic University in Rome.**

- **The name of Mother Teresa's first home for the dying was called *Nirmal Hriday* or Pure Heart.**

Thousands of letters have already been sent to the Pope requesting that Mother Teresa be made a saint.

"In twenty-five years, we have picked up from the streets of Calcutta 36,000 people and brought them to our hostels."

More Women in Profile

The following pages list a few more of the world's many humanitarians. All have devoted their lives to helping others. If you want to read more about them on your own, check the Suggested Reading list for more resources.

1920–1998
Bella Abzug
American Feminist

A lawyer by profession, Bella was the first Jewish woman to hold a seat in Congress. She was strongly against the Vietnam War, in which Americans fought the **communist** state of North Vietnam. Bella also supported the civil rights movement in the United States and was one of the leaders of the feminist movement, which called for equal rights for women.

Bella Abzug

1821–1912
Clara Barton
Founder of the American Red Cross

During the American **Civil War**, Clara brought supplies to the sick and wounded on the battlefield. She was appalled by the soldiers' suffering. In 1881, she organized the American branch of the Red Cross. At that time, the main aim of the Red Cross, which had been started in Switzerland in the 1860s, was to make sure that wounded soldiers and prisoners-of-war were treated well and given the care they needed.

1897–1980
Dorothy Day
American Social Worker

Dorothy helped found the Catholic Worker movement to help the poor. She also founded the *Catholic Worker* newspaper. During the Great Depression of the 1930s, Dorothy set up Houses of Hospitality in major cities throughout the United States. These houses gave people free meals and found shelter for the homeless.

1896–1944

Jozka Jaburkova

Czechoslovakian Feminist and Patriot

A journalist and children's writer, Jozka wanted better conditions for women in her country. She tried to get them better jobs and better pay, as well as good nurseries and schools for their children. When the Germans took over Czechoslovakia in 1939, Jozka was imprisoned in a **concentration camp**. Conditions were so terrible that she died there. In her home city of Prague, she is still considered a hero.

1929–

Elly Jansen

Dutch Social Worker

During her training as a nurse, Elly looked after people suffering from mental illness. She found that many of them were unhappy in the hospital and did not really need to be there. To make life better for them, Elly set up the Richmond Fellowship houses, where small groups of mentally ill patients could live together in pleasant surroundings. These houses now exist all over the world.

1876–1928

Eglantyne Jebb

English Founder of the Save the Children Fund

At the end of World War I, more than four million children were in danger of starving to death if they did not get food immediately. Eglantyne formed the Save the Children Fund in 1919 to help starving children in Europe. Soon, other countries all over the world raised money to feed the children. Eglantyne set up Save the Children International in 1920.

Eglantyne Jebb

1830–1917

Belva Ann Lockwood

American Lawyer and Peace Worker

Belva was the first woman to practice law before the United States Supreme Court. She led the way for other women lawyers. She campaigned to get equal rights for all people in the United States, including women, African Americans, and Native Americans. Belva was also deeply involved in the peace movement. She wanted the nations of the world to settle their problems by peaceful means, rather than fighting wars.

Belva Ann Lockwood

1837–1920

Anna Maria Mozzoni

Italian Feminist

Anna did much to improve the lives of the women of Italy. She founded an organization to defend Italian women's interests, and she wrote books and articles about the problems faced by women.

1902–1986

Alva Myrdal

Swedish Social Worker

Through her work at the United Nations, Alva did much to improve the lives of children. She campaigned for better children's education, free school meals, and aid for needy families. Alva also worked to bring about peace in the world. For nine years, she was a member of the United Nations Disarmament Committee.

1954–

Medha Patkar

Indian Environmentalist

Medha is India's best-known environmentalist. She has long campaigned against the building of huge dams. These projects cause large areas to be flooded, so that many people lose their homes. In 1998, Mehda and her followers successfully persuaded their government to stop building a huge dam on the sacred Narmada River in central India.

1923–

Susan Ryder

British Social Worker

Sue has devoted her life to helping people who have suffered greatly. She began by helping those who had been imprisoned in Nazi **concentration camps** during World War II. Later, she turned her attention to the elderly and to people with mental or physical difficulties. The Sue Ryder Foundation runs more than eighty stores to raise money for the many homes Sue has set up to help the disabled. Her homes care for people in Britain, India, Poland, and other countries. In honor of her work, she was made a baroness in 1978. As a baroness, she is known as Lady Ryder of Warsaw, but she prefers to be called Sue.

1927–

Shirley Smith

Australian Social Worker

An Australian Aborigine, Shirley has done much to help her people in the state of New South Wales. In 1971, she founded a legal service for Aborigines, and she gives advice and encouragement to people in prison. She also runs a home where single mothers can care for their babies. Mum Shirl, as she is known, even tried to win a seat in Parliament. She said, "Someone has to show young blacks how to become leaders."

1860–1945

Henrietta Szold

American Social Worker

Henrietta devoted her life to helping other Jewish people. In 1912, she founded Hadassah, the Jewish-American women's organization. She also did much to help Jewish children, both in the United States and in other countries around the world. When the Nazis came to power in Germany, Henrietta arranged for more than 100,000 Jewish children to be rescued, so that they escaped being killed in the **Holocaust**.

Henrietta Szold

Glossary

AIDS: a disease that destroys the body's ability to fight disease and infection

aristocrat: a member of the nobility

boycott: the refusal to buy or use

candid: a photograph taken without a person's knowledge

civil war: a war between people who live in the same country

colony: a region ruled by another country

communist: supporting communism—the belief that the state should control all property and methods of production

concentration camp: a camp where prisoners of war or enemies of the government are kept

convent: the place where nuns live and worship

governess: a woman who is employed to teach children in their home

Holocaust: the mass murder of many Jewish people during World War II

landmines: explosives laid in or on the ground so that they explode when someone steps or drives on them

migrant: someone who moves from one place to another

patron: a person who gives money or other support to a cause

pesticides: chemicals used to kill insects that destroy crops

polio: a virus that attacks the body's nerves and can cause permanent paralysis

saris: Indian women's traditional clothing made from a length of cloth wrapped around the body

socialism: the belief that the community, instead of a few individuals, should own and manage the land and money

strike: the refusal by employees to work until their demands are met

union: a group of workers who form a politically active group

Suggested Reading

Fraser, Antonia. *Heroes and Heroines*. London: Weidenfeld & Nicolson, 1980.

Golemba, Beverley. *Lesser-Known Women*. Boulder: Rienner, 1992.

James, T. Edward, ed. *Notable American Women 1607–1950*. Cambridge, MA: Belknap Press, 1971.

Keller, Helen. *The Story of My Life*. New York: Doubleday, 1954.

Morrow, Ann. *Princess*. London: Chapman's, 1991.

Raven, Susan, and Alison Weir. *Women of Achievement*. New York: Harmony, 1981.

Reilly Giff, Patricia. *Mother Teresa: Sister to the Poor*. New York: Viking Kestrel, 1986.

Saari, Peggy. *Prominent Women of the Twentieth Century*. Detroit: UXL, 1986.

Sickerman, Barbara, ed. *Notable American Women: The Modern Period*. Cambridge, MA: Belknap Press, 1980.

Telgen, Diane, and Jim Kamp, eds. *Notable Hispanic American Women*. Detroit: Gale Research, 1993.

Vardey, Lucinda. *Mother Teresa: A Simple Faith*. New York: Viking Kestrel, 1986.

Index

1 2 3 4 5 6 7 8 9 0 Printed in Canada 8 7 6 5 4 3 2 1 0 9